Pianoworks
Duets 2

compiled and arranged by
Janet and Alan Bullard

MUSIC DEPARTMENT

OXFORD
UNIVERSITY PRESS

UNIVERSITY PRESS

Great Clarendon Street, Oxford OX2 6DP, England

Oxford University Press is a department of the University of Oxford.
It furthers the University's aim of excellence in research, scholarship,
and education by publishing worldwide

3 5 7 9 10 8 6 4

ISBN 978–0–19–337836–0

Music and text origination by Julia Bovee
Printed in Great Britain on acid-free paper by
Halstan & Co. Ltd., Amersham, Bucks.

The *Pianoworks Duets* 2 CD was produced by Andrew McKenna Music.

Preface

Welcome to *Pianoworks Duets 2*.

We hope you will enjoy this opportunity to play piano duets with a friend or teacher.

The suggested hints and tips for duet playing found in *Pianoworks Duets 1* also apply to this book. Some pedalling has been indicated for the secondo player, but this can be omitted if desired. The suggested fingerings should suit most players, but they are only suggestions—every hand is different.

With this book we have provided a digitized CD of the individual parts (sometimes with slower and faster versions) so that you can play each part with a 'virtual' pianist. Although not completely representative of a live performance, we hope the CD will be useful for practice, and that you will find the opportunity to duet with a 'real' pianist as well.

Good luck, and enjoy your duet playing!

JANET AND ALAN BULLARD

Contents

All pieces are original compositions or arrangements by Janet and Alan Bullard.

Prélude

from *Te Deum*

Marc-Antoine Charpentier
(1643–1704)

Often performed on celebratory occasions, the instrumental prelude to this setting of the Te Deum was written when Charpentier was Master of Music at the Church of St Louis in Paris. Charpentier was also an operatic composer, and he brought the grand, dramatic feel of his operas to his sacred works. Aim for bold playing with confident finger work to convey this style.

Prélude

from *Te Deum*

Marc-Antoine Charpentier
(1643–1704)

Nocturne No. 3

'Liebestraum'

Franz Liszt
(1811–86)

* Pause: 2nd time only

Originally for solo piano, Nocturne No. 3 is one of Liszt's most popular works, displaying his gift for expressively flowing melody and rich harmony. In this version the melody begins in the secondo and later appears in the primo part; let the tune sing out, keeping the accompanying quavers in the background.

Nocturne No. 3

'Liebestraum'

Franz Liszt
(1811–86)

* Pause: 2nd time only

Spring

from *The Four Seasons*

Antonio Vivaldi
(1678–1741)

The violin concertos of *Le quattro stagioni* ('The Four Seasons') were originally written to accompany four descriptive sonnets. The first of these begins: 'Spring has come, and birds greet it with cheerful songs'. To communicate this character, play with energy and enjoy the contrasting dynamics. A shorter version of this piece can be created by returning to bar 4 on the repeat (instead of bar 1), and by finishing either on the first beat of bar 10 or at the *Fine*.

Spring

from *The Four Seasons*

Antonio Vivaldi
(1678–1741)

track **7** Secondo part only

Violin Concerto
theme from the second movement

Felix Mendelssohn
(1809–47)

Mendelssohn's lovely Violin Concerto combines the elegance of the Classical era with the drama of the Romantic period. In this arrangement of the second movement, aim to create an expressive ebb and flow in the music, perhaps aided by touches of pedal. The secondo staccatos in bars 20–1 represent pizzicato cellos and basses in the original.

Violin Concerto
theme from the second movement

Felix Mendelssohn
(1809–47)

Gymnopédie No. 1

Erik Satie
(1866–1925)

Satie's delicate Gymnopédie No. 1 was originally written for solo piano but has since been arranged for many different ensembles. Well-graded crescendos and diminuendos in the primo part will help to create an atmospheric performance.

Gymnopédie No. 1

Erik Satie
(1866–1925)

Hallelujah Chorus

from *Messiah*

George Frideric Handel
(1685–1759)

As one of the most famous pieces of choral music in the world, Handel's joyous 'Hallelujah Chorus' needs little introduction. To create a rhythmic and energetic performance, slightly detach the quavers and semiquavers.

track **12** Primo part only

PRIMO

Hallelujah Chorus
from *Messiah*

George Frideric Handel
(1685–1759)

House in the clouds

Alan Bullard
(b. 1947)

Aim for a gentle, dreamy mood in this evocative piece. Placing your hands forward over the keyboard will make it easier for the fingers to reach the black notes and achieve an expressive legato.

House in the clouds

Alan Bullard
(b. 1947)

March

from *Così fan tutte*

Wolfgang Amadeus Mozart
(1756–91)

This rousing operatic march is sung by a chorus of townspeople as the two young heroes deceive their girlfriends by pretending to go off to battle. To create the desired military tone, play the rhythms tightly and precisely.

track 16 Primo part only

PRIMO

March
from *Così fan tutte*

Wolfgang Amadeus Mozart
(1756–91)

Afton Water

Trad. Scottish

Setting a text by Robert Burns, this traditional Scottish song is a gentle lullaby sung to the River Afton in Ayrshire. To evoke this scene, play the rippling quavers in the right hand of the secondo part very gently, allowing the primo melody to float above. Some subtle pedalling will help to enrich the texture.

Afton Water

Trad. Scottish

Minuet

from Quintet in E major, Op. 13 No. 5

Luigi Boccherini
(1743–1805)

Born in Italy, Boccherini spent most of his working life in Spain, where he wrote more than a hundred string quintets. This graceful dance is by far his most popular, and it has often been used in films and television programmes. Set a steady tempo, without hurrying, and carefully count the tied notes in the primo left-hand.

Minuet

from Quintet in E major, Op. 13 No. 5

Luigi Boccherini
(1743–1805)

All things are quite silent

Trad. English

Dating back to the Napoleonic Wars, this lament is sung by a young wife whose husband has been forced into the navy. In bars 1–11 and 22–5, the sustained notes in the primo part will provide an evocative accompaniment to the haunting secondo melody.

All things are quite silent

Trad. English

The open ties in bars 1–11 and 22–5 indicate that the fingers should hold each note until it is replayed.

Panis angelicus
(Bread of the Angels)

César Franck
(1822–90)

Originally written for tenor, harp, cello, double bass, and organ, Franck's setting of St Thomas Aquinas's hymn text has become one of his most popular works. Keep the accompanying quavers in the secondo part steady and even throughout, taking care when they pass from the right hand to the left hand in bars 8–9. Note that in bar 10 the secondo part copies the primo melody, creating a canon between the two players. Some gentle pedalling is appropriate, but listen carefully to avoid blurring the sound.

Panis angelicus
(Bread of the Angels)

César Franck
(1822–90)

Crown Imperial
Coronation March

William Walton
(1902–83)

First performed at the coronation of King George VI in 1937, this stirring march has now become a favourite at many royal occasions. Let the music flow in the opening section, and make the rhythms very precise in the final bars, where primo and secondo need to take care not to get in each other's way! For a shorter version of this piece, finish the performance on the first beat of the second time bar, holding the first chord as a minim.

Crown Imperial

Coronation March

William Walton
(1902–83)

Symphony No. 3

theme from the third movement

Johannes Brahms
(1833–97)

This symphony was first performed in 1883 by the Vienna Philharmonic Orchestra, conducted by Hans Richter. At the beginning of this arrangement the wonderful cello melody appears in the secondo part; allow this line to project smoothly by using a warm, legato tone, with delicate playing in the primo part.

Symphony No. 3

theme from the third movement

Johannes Brahms
(1833–97)

Moderate and flowing

SECONDO

track 29 Secondo part only

The Easy Winners

Ragtime two-step

Scott Joplin
(c.1867–1917)

Although the syncopated style of this popular rag was innovative for its time, the 'oom-pah' accompaniment patterns reveal its link to nineteenth-century popular music. Joplin stated that ragtime should not be played too fast, so keep the secondo quavers steady, allowing the primo part to be played neatly and delicately.

The Easy Winners

Ragtime two-step

Scott Joplin
(c.1867–1917)

Chanson de matin
(Morning Song)

Edward Elgar
(1857–1934)

Originally scored for violin and piano, this elegant work is one of several salon pieces that Elgar wrote towards the end of the nineteenth century. *Sonore* (or *sonoramente*) was one of Elgar's favourite instructions: the primo player should use a rich, sonorous tone for the left-hand melody that begins in bar 25.

Chanson de matin
(Morning Song)

Edward Elgar
(1857–1934)

Piano Concerto No. 1

theme from the first movement

Pyotr Il'yich Tchaikovsky
(1840–93)

The exhilarating opening of Tchaikovsky's First Piano Concerto never fails to grip audiences. To create this dramatic effect, emphasize the accents and tenutos at the beginning, and allow the primo melody (played by strings in the original) to sing out powerfully. Towards the end both players should use a lighter touch for the triplet accompaniment in the right hand.

Piano Concerto No. 1
theme from the first movement

Pyotr Il'yich Tchaikovsky
(1840–93)

The Elephant

from *The Carnival of the Animals*

Camille Saint-Saëns
(1835–1921)

This is one of the most popular movements in Saint-Saëns's colourful menagerie. Be careful not to play it too fast, and make sure the staccatos and accents are crisp to give it plenty of character.

The Elephant
from *The Carnival of the Animals*

Camille Saint-Saëns
(1835–1921)

Habanera

from *Carmen*

Georges Bizet
(1838–75)

Sung by the cigarette girl Carmen, this sinuously seductive song captures the soldier Don José's attention, changing both his and Carmen's futures forever. In the secondo part, keep the characteristic habanera rhythm steady throughout; the primo melody should be played legato, with unhurried triplets. For full dramatic effect, allow plenty of time on the pause just before the end.

Habanera

from *Carmen*

Georges Bizet
(1838–75)

track 39 Secondo part only

The Shepherds' Farewell

from *L'enfance du Christ*

Hector Berlioz
(1803–69)

Berlioz's gentle Christmas lullaby has long been a favourite with audiences. Despite the 3/8 time signature, it should be played slowly and calmly to allow the subtleties of the chromatic passages to take effect.

The Shepherds' Farewell

from *L'enfance du Christ*

Hector Berlioz
(1803–69)

Wild Swan Tango

Alan Bullard
(b. 1947)

With more than a glance towards Tchaikovsky's ballet *Swan Lake*, this tango calls for a confident rhythmic drive throughout. The secondo player needs to be ready to change from accompanist to soloist in bar 36, while the primo player turns the page.

Wild Swan Tango

Alan Bullard
(b. 1947)

SECONDO